US MILITARY CAREERS

US MARINE CORPS

BY GAIL RADLEY

CONTENT CONSULTANT
Major Ralia Bouska, US Marine Corps
Commandant of the Marine Corps Fellows
The Fletcher School, Tufts University

An Imprint of Abdo Publishing | abdobooks.com

ABDOBOOKS.COM

Published by Abdo Publishing, a division of ABDO, PO Box 398166, Minneapolis, Minnesota 55439.

Printed in the United States of America, North Mankato, Minnesota.
042020
092020

Cover Photo: Shutterstock Images
Interior Photos: Lance Cpl. Dalton S. Swanbeck/US Marine Corps/Defense Visual Information Distribution Service, 4–5; Cpl. Scott Jenkins/US Marine Corps/Defense Visual Information Distribution Service, 7; Lance Cpl. Joshua Sechser/US Marine Corps/Defense Visual Information Distribution Service, 9, 26–27, 46; North Wind Picture Archives, 12–13, 16; Everett - Art/Shutterstock Images, 14; James Martenhoff/AP Images, 21; Kemberly Groue/US Air Force/Defense Visual Information Distribution Service, 24; Lance Cpl. Joshua Sechser/US Marine Corps/Defense Visual Information; Cpl. Tawanya Norwood/US Marine Corps/Defense Visual Information Distribution Service, 30; Shutterstock Images, 35; Sgt. James A. Guillory/US Marine Corps/Defense Visual Information Distribution Service, 36; Lance Cpl. Zachary T. Beatty/US Marine Corps/Defense Visual Information Distribution Service, 38; Sgt. Kyle C. Talbot/US Marine Corps/Defense Visual Information Distribution Service, 40–41; Cpl. Isaac Cantrell/US Marine Corps/Defense Visual Information Distribution Service, 43; Cpl. Drew Tech/US Marine Corps/Defense Visual Information Distribution Service, 45; Staff Sgt. Ezekiel R. Kitandwe/US Marine Corps/Defense Visual Information Distribution Service, 52–53; Lance Cpl. Alexa Hernandez/US Marine Corps/Defense Visual Information Distribution Service, 56; Cpl. Jodson B. Graves/US Marine Corps/Defense Visual Information Distribution Service, 60–61; Staff Sgt. Mark E. Morrow Jr./US Marine Corps/Defense Visual Information Distribution Service, 62; Gunnery Sgt. Ricardo A. Gomez/US Marine Corps/Defense Visual Information Distribution Service, 66; Lance Cpl. John Hall/US Marine Corps/Defense Visual Information Distribution Service, 68–69; Lance Cpl. Harrison Rakhshani/US Marine Corps/Defense Visual Information Distribution Service, 71; Lance Cpl. Kerstin Roberts/US Marine Corps/Defense Visual Information Distribution Service, 73; Lance Cpl. Angelo K. Garavito/US Marine Corps/Defense Visual Information Distribution Service, 74; Lance Cpl. Elias E. Pimentel III/US Marine Corps/Defense Visual Information Distribution Service, 80–81; Lance Cpl. Tawanya Norwood/US Marine Corps/Defense Visual Information Distribution Service, 83; Sgt. Robert Knapp/US Marine Corps/Defense Visual Information Distribution Service, 88–89; Sgt. Jessica Quezada/US Marine Corps/Defense Visual Information Distribution Service, 92; Lance Cpl. Heather Atherton//US Marine Corps/Defense Visual Information Distribution Service, 97

Editor: Charly Haley
Series Designer: Nikki Nordby

LIBRARY OF CONGRESS CONTROL NUMBER: 2019954354

PUBLISHER'S CATALOGING-IN-PUBLICATION DATA

Names: Radley, Gail, author.
Title: US Marine Corps / by Gail Radley
Description: Minneapolis, Minnesota : Abdo Publishing, 2021 | Series: US military careers | Includes online resources and index.
Identifiers: ISBN 9781532192296 (lib. bdg.) | ISBN 9781098210199 (ebook)
Subjects: LCSH: Marines--Juvenile literature. | Members of the Armed Forces--Juvenile literature. | Military power--Juvenile literature. | United States. Marine Corps--History--Juvenile literature. | Armed Forces--Juvenile literature.
Classification: DDC 355.12--dc23

CONTENTS

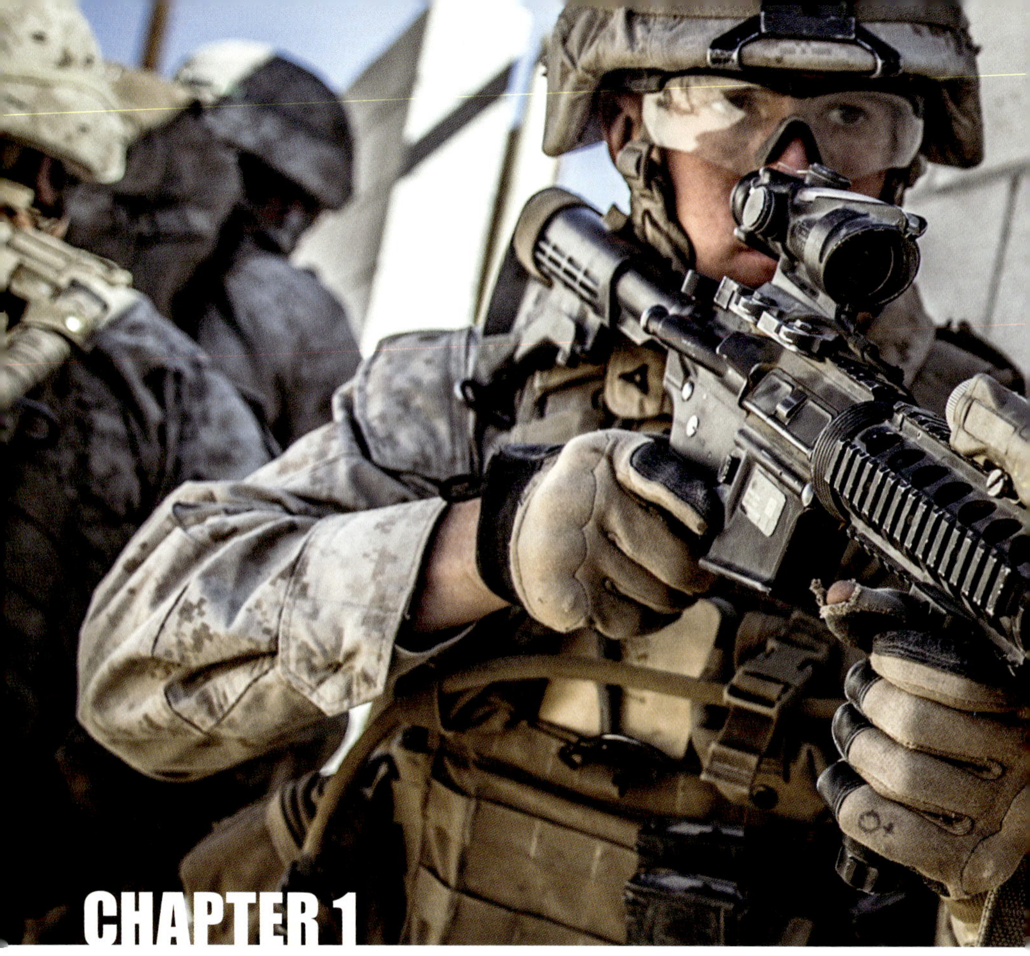

CHAPTER 1

MEET THE MARINES

A corporal pressed against the building, waiting for the signal to move. The US Army had the Iraqi city of Fallujah surrounded as planned. But that meant some 3,000 to 4,000 enemy fighters were trapped inside the city. The US Marine Corps had swept through the city before, but the enemy had returned stronger than ever. Enemy soldiers could be hiding in

Marines train for combat in many environments, including in cities.

any business or home. It was the marines' job to help their allies, the Iraqi forces, take back the city.

The corporal and a private had just darted through a rain of fire in a courtyard. Now the corporal was trying to steady his breathing. He hoped the enemy couldn't see them now—that they weren't in some insurgent's sights. He glanced over his shoulder at the men behind him. It looked like someone from the team was missing. Where was the lance corporal? Hadn't he made it through the courtyard? They needed to move forward.

Maybe the lance corporal was holed up in another doorway. He'd race in to support them from another angle. The lance corporal had that way of popping up where people least expected—and most needed—him.

The corporal stepped toward the door and gave it a hard kick. He walked into the empty room, his weapon ready, the private by his side. The corporal scanned the room as the private crept toward an adjoining room. The corporal darted toward the stairs. It seemed eerily quiet. Suddenly shots rang out. The corporal spotted two insurgents behind an overturned couch in another room. He returned fire until theirs stopped and the enemies lay motionlessly, blood from their wounds pooling on the floor around them.

The corporal shouted, ducking as a spray of bullets came from upstairs. When it stopped, the corporal took to the stairs, the private at his heels. The insurgents scattered into the several upstairs rooms as the marines returned fire. The private disappeared to his right, following them. The corporal took the room ahead. He spotted several propane tanks and plastic explosives. If he fired now, they'd all be blown to the sky, he realized. The click of a weapon out of ammunition drew his attention. Suddenly an enemy fighter dove toward the open window. The corporal lunged for him, using the end of his rifle

★ Dangerous missions require marines to work well in teams.

to hit the fighter's head. Unlike the US marines, the insurgent fighter wore no helmet. He sank to the floor in pain.

The corporal checked the other two rooms and met the private downstairs. The building seemed to be secure. Another marine entered. "Clear out," he said. "Air support is coming."

The corporal remembered the lance corporal as they left. He trotted back to the courtyard. It was quiet for a moment. Then he saw the lance corporal slumped over a few yards away. The corporal's heart raced as he ran toward the lance corporal.

SEMPER FI

The US Marine Corps adopted in 1883 the Latin phrase *semper fidelis*, meaning "always faithful," as its motto. Colonel Charles Grymes McCawley chose the motto, but apparently he never explained why. While no one knows McCawley's exact reasoning, his choice came at a time when the marine corps was looking for more spiffy uniforms and symbols. The Latin phrase has a history of use in Europe, including being used by some militaries in the 1600s. The US Marine Corps has continued to use McCawley's chosen motto, often shortening it to *Semper fi* (SEM-per fye).

The corporal kept thinking, *Not him.* Turning the lance corporal over, the corporal saw the blood oozing from beneath his flak jacket. The lance corporal's eyes fluttered open. He gave the corporal a weak smile. "I was hoping you might come around," he said.

"*Semper fi*, brother," muttered the corporal, helping the lance corporal up. "Hold on, now."

The lance corporal would survive, the corporal told himself. One day they'd swap stories about the second battle of Fallujah in late 2004, one of the fiercest battles of the Iraq War (2003–2011).

THE MARINES' MISSION

Some people think of members of the US Marine Corps by their nickname "soldiers of the sea." The marines began as the US Navy's ground troops in 1775. The navy specialized in handling ships and sea battles; the marines' duty was to hit the shore

A group of marines operates a small boat in the Philippine Sea.

fighting. The two forces traveled aboard the same vessels. The name *marine* comes from *mer,* the French word for "sea." So there is a strong connection between marines and the sea. However, today marines fight "on land, sea, and air," the US Marine Corps website states, adding that their mission is to "win our nation's battles swiftly and aggressively in times of crisis."[1]

When other people think of the marines, they might imagine a stereotypical picture of camouflage-clad men clutching rifles and darting through jungles or desert sands. That picture may match reality sometimes. But the US Marine Corps also includes women darting to their duty. Women have been in the marines since Opha Mae Johnson enlisted to become a marine clerk in 1918. It wasn't until 2013, though, that the US Congress decided women could serve in combat roles, planting their combat boots and carrying their M4 rifles on any battleground anywhere.

Still, there is more to the marines than either of these pictures suggests. The US Marine Corps is one of six US military branches. The others are the US Army, the US Navy, the US Air Force, the US Coast Guard, and the US Space Force. The work of the marine corps is widely varied, with marines stationed all over the world. In addition to defending the United States by land, sea, and air, the marines also conduct humanitarian aid

MARINE CORPS FLAG

The marines carried several different flags before they settled on their current gold-and-scarlet banner in 1925. At the center of the marine corps' flag is the same emblem that marines wear on their uniforms—the eagle, globe, and anchor (EGA). The eagle is a symbol of the United States and the marines' pledge to defend their country. The eagle holds a banner with the marine motto, *Semper fidelis*, while a larger banner below the EGA announces the name "United States Marine Corps."

The center of the emblem shows a globe, symbolizing that the marines serve around the world. The Western Hemisphere faces forward, however, as that is where the early marines served most. The anchor is a nod to the marines' ties with the US Navy. The rope looped around the anchor symbolizes the marine corps' permanence—it is here to stay.

LEATHERNECKS AND JARHEADS

The marines have some odd nicknames. One of them is *leatherneck*. This goes back to the American Revolutionary War (1775–1783), when marines wore green coats with beige trim and pants, along with leather collars, useful against sword blows to the neck. The collars also encouraged marines to keep their heads high in parades. Navy sailors, seeing the sturdy collars, dubbed the marines "leathernecks." Although they gave up the collars in the 1870s, the nickname continues today. Another nickname, picked up during World War II (1939–1945), is *jarhead*. The marines' formal uniforms, known as dress blues, have high collars. Sailors tried to insult the marines by suggesting they looked like they'd been stuffed into Mason jars. Rather than being upset, the marines adopted the nickname.

and disaster relief missions. Whether it's working with Nepalese soldiers to deliver supplies after an earthquake, helping to restore a school in Trinidad and Tobago, or evacuating North Carolinians sheltered in a fire station after Hurricane Florence, the US Marines are there.

CHAPTER 2

THE HISTORY OF THE US MARINE CORPS

It was no small task for the American colonies to fight for independence from well-established Great Britain. The American Revolutionary War (1775–1783) effort began with militias. A ragtag group of marines was pulled from the militias to take to the sea. Most knew little about ships.

Americans fought the British on land and sea during the Revolutionary War.

By November 10, 1775, though, the colonies' Second Continental Congress decided the coastlines needed to be protected by trained seamen and warships. Thus began the Continental marines. More than 2,000 marines, including 131 officers, served alongside the country's Continental navy.[1]

When the colonies won their freedom in 1783, the Continental marines and navy were dismissed. Soon, however, the newly formed United States realized it needed a standing military, particularly a navy to protect its trading ships. In 1798, President

★ President John Adams signed a congressional act in 1798 that officially formed the US Marine Corps.

John Adams ordered the Continental marines to re-form as the US Marine Corps. They were soon sent to battle against France and then against pirates at Tripoli, in what is now Libya. After fighting off the pirates, the marines, led by Lieutenant Presley O'Bannon, also helped restore Prince Hamet Bey as the ruler of Tripoli. Grateful for their heroism, the prince presented O'Bannon with a sword. A replica of that sword would become a regular part of the marines' dress uniform.

FIGHTING ON LAND AND SEA

By 1834, the marines' ability to fight on land as well as at sea was clear. Congress saw the marines and navy as "sister services," making them separate units under one department.[2] The marines would serve as the navy's fighting unit on the ground. The navy, in turn, would fulfill the marines' need for medical workers, chaplains, and other noncombat personnel.

The marines fought in the Mexican-American War (1846–1848) and guarded Mexico's presidential palace at Montezuma. The American Civil War (1861–1865) broke out following the decision of most southern states to form a separate nation. Known as the Confederacy, the rebelling southern states sought to maintain the enslavement of black people. The mostly northern, or Union, states fought to end slavery and preserve the United States as a whole. Seventeen marines were awarded Medals of Honor for their efforts.[3] These medals, established in 1861, acknowledge acts of courage and are the highest honors given to military members.

The marines went on to fight in small wars around the world during the late 1800s. Their experience broadened as the US Marine Corps took over the island nation of Haiti in 1915 to guard American commercial and political interests. The marines occupied Haiti for 19 years, and in that process they killed thousands of Haitians who fought for their independence.[4]

★ An illustration shows US military forces, including marines, landing on the coast of Mexico during the Mexican-American War.

In 1916, US Marines attempted a takeover of Haiti's neighbor, the Dominican Republic. There, they also met resistance from local military fighters as well as from ordinary citizens. Six years later, neither side could claim victory. The Dominicans agreed to surrender, provided the marines left, which they eventually did in 1924.

From these and other small wars, the marines learned valuable lessons in guerrilla warfare. In this type of fighting, there is no clear battlefield; fighting might spark anywhere. Forming relationships with the local people was important to these marines, so that the locals wouldn't side with rebel fighters. Charging in, guns blazing, as the marines were used to doing, was not productive in these situations. Instead, the 1940 *Small Wars Manual*, detailing lessons learned by the marines, argued, "tolerance, sympathy, and kindness should be the keynote to our relationship with the mass of the population."[5]

WORLD WARS

World War I (1914–1918) would be a major test for the US Marine Corps. The United States got involved in the conflict in 1917. Secretary of War Newton Baker wasn't eager for the still-small marine corps to enter what he thought should be a "US Army show."[6] The marines had fewer men than the army. Some people felt the marine corps was unnecessary and should be abolished. The marines, however, were eager to uphold their recruiting slogan First to Fight. They won their chance. When the marines joined the army to fight in France, the army's General John J. Pershing was distressed to find the marines better trained and looking sharper than his own men.

As army leadership was pushing for the marine corps to be abolished, *Chicago Tribune* reporter Floyd Gibbons thrilled American audiences at home with vivid stories of marines in action during World War I. As many marines died in the war, news of their bravery and successes helped to build a stronger reputation for the US Marine Corps as a whole. World War I also

THE CODE TALKERS

In World War II, the marines recruited members of the Native American nations to send and receive coded military messages. Because so few people knew Native American languages, they would serve as an effective basis for hard-to-break codes. The marines created a code school for intensive training of 400 Navajos as well as Comanches, Hopis, and Meskwakis. These marines, as members of different Native American nations, worked together to assign various Native American words to military terms. For example, the Comanche word for "turtle" meant *tank,* and the Hopi word for "houses on water" meant *ships*. For information that wasn't especially sensitive, the Navajos simply spoke in their own language. These Native American marines also learned to work with electronic communication equipment in battle. They used this technology and the codes they had developed to deliver critical information that helped the United States win the war. Their codes were never broken.

gave the marines battle experience in large-scale warfare, as opposed to the small wars they had engaged in previously.

Still, by 1941, 89 percent of young military enlistees chose other branches of the service over the marines.[7] Retired marine captain Aaron B. O'Connell writes, "Before World War II the United States Marine Corps was tiny, unpopular, and institutionally disadvantaged."[8] The marines made up just 3 percent of the military.[9] Because it was linked with the navy, the marine corps couldn't create its own budget and decide how to spend its money. Even more troubling, the marines had a reputation for being rowdy and undisciplined. Marines were fiercely proud, and their insistence on their own way of doing things somewhat isolated them from other military branches and likely contributed to this reputation.

World War II began with German dictator Adolf Hitler's 1939 invasion of Poland. The United Kingdom and France rose to defend Poland. The United States held back from entering the fighting until Japan, an ally of Germany, launched a surprise attack on a US naval base in Hawaii's Pearl Harbor in 1941. Japan's aim was to cripple US Navy fleets, preventing the United States from responding to its expansion into Southeast Asia.

With more than 2,400 people killed and 18 ships sunk or disabled during the attack on Pearl Harbor, the United States

AFRICAN AMERICANS IN WORLD WAR II

As the United States ramped up for World War II in 1941, the country was still racially segregated. But, like other military branches, the marines were short on men. With much pressure and persuasion—and against the wishes of the US Marine Corps commandant—President Franklin D. Roosevelt ordered that African Americans be allowed to enlist in the military. Once the marine corps was open to them, thousands of black men stepped up. To start, the marines selected 1,200 from among them.[10]

When the recruits arrived at Montfort Point, North Carolina, to train, they found empty grounds that were mosquito-infested and inadequate, even though the brand-new, fully operational Camp Lejeune—reserved for white recruits—was nearby. The recruits' first job was to build their own camp. Although the first training officers were white, by 1945, there were black officers in charge. Today, African Americans are 12 percent of the marine corps, totaling 21,000 active duty marines.[11]

could no longer hold back.[12] By the next day, the United States, too, was at war. While other US military branches went to Europe to help the country's allies fight against Germany, most marines headed for the Pacific to capture Japanese-held islands. The marines established military bases on these islands and battled Japanese soldiers. Many marines were injured or killed fighting in the war.

KOREA, VIETNAM, AND BEYOND

In 1950, not long after World War II, Communist North Korea invaded South Korea, starting the Korean War (1950–1953). Along with other military forces, the US Marines were sent to help South Korea. It took only five days of close fighting to back North Korea out of South Korea's capital city, Seoul. From there, marines participated in other battles throughout South Korea until the war ended. More than 4,200 marines died in the effort.[13]

The Vietnam War (1954–1975) also involved Communist armies attempting to take over the country. As in Korea, the US military went to Vietnam to help fight against the Communists. The Vietnam War era was particularly difficult for the US military overall, and the marines were not an exception. For the first time, television brought footage of battles into American living rooms, showing the brutality of war. The seemingly endless

★ US Marines fight against Communist guerrilla soldiers in 1951 during the Korean War.

nature of the war, the mounting casualties, and increasing costs frustrated the American public. Because it was a civil war in Vietnam, Americans grew increasingly upset with their own country's involvement, saying it was not the United States' business to interfere and that it was immoral. Marines, along with army soldiers, navy sailors, and members of the air force, were often greeted with disrespect upon returning home from the war. They were not made to feel like returning heroes.

Toward the war's end and after, enlistment in the marine corps dropped. (By 1973, the draft, which required many young men to enter the US military—usually the army—had ended and all US military service had become voluntary.) Many of those who did enlist in the marines around this time arrived without the skills, fitness, and determination of previous recruits. Moreover, once again, there were calls to disband the marine corps. But the marines rallied. General Robert E. Cushman Jr. announced, "We are pulling our heads out of the jungle and getting back to the amphibious business."[14] The marine corps would refocus on its mission of fighting by both land and sea, rather than its guerrilla warfare efforts.

WAR ON TERROR

Meanwhile, tensions were growing between Middle Eastern countries and Western countries. In 1983, the US embassy in Beirut, Lebanon, was bombed and destroyed by terrorists. Later that year, a terrorist truck-bomb destroyed US military barracks in Beirut. Of the 241 members of the US military who died that day, 220 were marines.[15]

Years later, the United States faced a harrowing attack on its own soil on September 11, 2001. Foreign terrorists from the group al-Qaida hijacked and then crashed four passenger airplanes into several buildings, killing nearly 3,000 people.[16]

They hit the World Trade Center's Twin Towers in New York City and the Pentagon, which houses the US Department of Defense, in Washington, DC. The attack prompted the United States to launch the War on Terror. This was to be a military campaign, with the cooperation of other nations, to find and stop terrorist activity around the world.

A month after the September 11 attack, US military forces went to Afghanistan to remove the terrorist group that had taken over, called the Taliban, which was said to have sheltered

COMBAT OBSCURA

The US Marine Corps website stresses that the marine corps builds "pride, honor, and integrity" among its personnel. But a 2019 documentary, *Combat Obscura,* shows that marines don't always reach those high goals. Filmmaker Miles Lagoze, a former combat videographer, explained, "I think we're at a point as veterans that we want to show war as it is. We're kind of sick of the hero-worshipping."[17]

Combat videographers film war for study and publicity. While serving in Afghanistan in 2011, Lagoze was tasked with filming marines training Afghan troops to protect their own country from terrorists. Lagoze was supposed to avoid filming the blood, gore, and innocent lives taken. But his documentary captures the violence of war, along with a range of disturbing behaviors by marines. The film shows marines taunting children, disrespecting Afghan citizens, and blowing up homes, sometimes mistakenly. "While we were there, we created an almost uninhabitable environment for the Afghan civilians," Lagoze said.[18] While US Marine Corps officials responded to Lagoze's film by saying it does not reflect the majority of marines, Lagoze maintains that the film is an accurate picture of his own deployment to Afghanistan.

★ A US Marine Corps staff sergeant, *right*, and a US Navy sailor hold up an American flag during a memorial ceremony for victims of the September 11 terrorist attacks.

al-Qaida. Soon after, the lengthy Iraq War (2003–2011) began as the United States fought to stop former Iraqi president Saddam Hussein's abuse of the country's minority groups, threats of weapons of mass destruction, and harboring of terrorists.

Two decades later, the United States is still engaged in the War on Terror. The terrorist threat has moved around the globe, taking the military to 40 percent of the world's countries.[19] And the marines, like other branches of the service, have been in the thick of it. Marines have found themselves fighting in cities, fighting house-to-house, and in close combat. It is unconventional warfare in which the enemy does not wear a uniform and blends in easily with the population, and danger looms up suddenly in the form of a roadside bomb or sniper fire.

CHAPTER 3

THE US MARINE CORPS TODAY

"You don't join the Marines," announces the US Marine Corps website. "You become one."[1] The point is, the title *marine* is something that enlistees must earn. It is earned through tough training and hard work. There are several ways

Marines can operate aboard ships or aircraft.

to become a marine and many reasons that people choose to do so.

There are some requirements a person must meet to step onto that path. Typically, enlisted recruits commit to four to six years of active duty. They must be between 17 and 28. They must be legal residents of the United States, high school graduates, and able to pass a physical exam. They also must pass the Armed Services Vocational Aptitude Battery (ASVAB), a test that all incoming military recruits must take. Participating in a

Junior Reserve Officers' Training Corps (JROTC) program in high school is not required, but it is helpful in acquainting future marines with the work and expectations ahead of them.

GETTING STARTED

Upon acceptance into the marine corps, recruits go through training. Those wanting to become officers will go to Officer Candidate School or the US Naval Academy. The entry requirements for officers, however, are higher than for enlisted personnel. This is because officers lead enlisted marines and sometimes make high-level organizational decisions. An officer candidate must be at least 18 and not older than 27. The candidate must also be a US citizen and either have earned a bachelor's degree or be a full-time university or college student.

College students hoping to begin their marine careers as officers often start with the marine curriculum in the Naval Reserve Officers' Training Corps (NROTC) program. They participate in the program while taking regular college courses and following the requirements of their chosen majors. The NROTC program includes classes in American military affairs and national security policy. The marine corps also offers college scholarships to qualified students.

It's also possible to be a part-time marine. The Marine Reserves is composed of well-trained marines who are ready to go into active duty in times of war or emergency. In the meantime, they work in other jobs or attend school. They keep their skills up by training one weekend each month and by attending a two-week training session each year.

Private First Class Brooke L. Jalbert had the same motivation as many people who join the marines. She had had trouble figuring out what she wanted to do after high school. She tried college, but it didn't suit her. "I wanted to be a part of something bigger than myself," she explains, "something that will show me how to succeed and become a better human being."[2] After graduating from marine boot camp, Jalbert says her platoon feels like family.

Like new recruits in all military branches, marine recruits begin with basic training, or boot camp. After completing basic training, most new marines go to Marine Combat Training (MCT). Some marines are fond of the motto "Every marine a

FURTHER EDUCATION

Many people are drawn to the marines because of the benefits that come with the job. While some learn marine skills through high school and college ROTC programs, others are able to further their education as a benefit of being in the marines. The Military Academic Skills Program helps marines brush up on math and reading skills while in the service. This is great for marines who are weak in those areas. It readies some of them for college, which the marine corps will pay for if the student is on active duty. The marine corps even partners with colleges to provide online courses wherever the marines are.

★ Two marines carry part of an unmanned aircraft system during a training exercise. Marines continue training throughout their military careers.

rifleman," as almost all marines are trained in combat and many marine positions are related to the battlefield. But there are still more than 180 specialties available to marines, and they don't all involve combat. Marines who are headed for combat as part of the infantry spend 51 days training at the School of Infantry, while the others just get battle basics in the 22-day MCT.[3] After combat training, the marines are off to specialized training for their specific jobs. Marines can choose their jobs, but if there are no openings in the relevant training program, they may be assigned elsewhere. The length of specialized training depends on the job. After their specialized training is complete, the marines head to work at their duty stations.

RANKS

All US military branches organize their personnel by rank. Enlisted marines are divided into junior enlisted ranks, noncommissioned officers (NCOs), staff noncommissioned officers (SNCOs), and warrant officers, for those with particular specialties. Ranked above the enlisted marines are commissioned officers.

Junior enlisted ranks begin with the private, a graduate of basic training. Six months later, most are moved into private first class for simply using their skills and following orders. Similarly, nine months of service usually guarantees a move to lance corporal, with approval from a commander. At this stage, marines begin working on leadership skills. Only those who show leadership potential move on to become NCOs.

FEMALE ENGAGEMENT TEAMS

Women make up 8 percent of the US Marine Corps.[4] While all military jobs are open to men and women, the marines have found that there are some missions only women can complete. This is why the marine corps has Female Engagement Teams (FETs). Some marine corps missions involve working with locals in foreign countries to improve conditions or to gather information. However, cultural differences can interfere with this. In some countries, women aren't supposed to meet with men who aren't their relatives. In situations like this, the specially trained women of the marine corps' FETs can establish important relationships that male marines simply cannot.

NCOs are in charge of lower-ranking marines. They are expected to teach skills and be role models. The NCO ranks are corporal, then sergeant. Moving into these ranks requires marines to demonstrate solid leadership qualities. Moving from sergeant into an SNCO position requires approval from a selection board.

SNCO positions are for enlisted personnel who want to advance in the ranks but probably do not intend to become commissioned officers. SNCOs run from staff sergeant (a leader of lower-ranked marines including lower sergeants) to master gunnery sergeant (a leader with strong technical skills) and sergeant major, an adviser to the commanders.

UNIFORMS

The marines have several uniforms. Camouflage is the standard, worn during combat or when overseas, as well as during training. Officially called the Marine Corps Combat Utility Uniform, "cammies" are typically in shades of green to blend in with woodlands. A white-and-gray pattern works better for cold environments, and for deserts, tan and browns. The eagle, globe, and anchor symbol is hidden in the camouflage.

The marines are most famous for their elegant "dress blues," worn on formal occasions. The bright red stripe on the leg of officers' uniforms, called the "blood stripe," honors marines lost in battle. While wearing dress blues, commissioned officers carry a traditional sword known as the Mameluke and noncommissioned officers carry the NCO sword, both in recognition of service in combat.

The warrant officer program is another route into higher rank for marines without college degrees. A warrant officer represents the best in his or her specific job and is considered "a technical expert," says Chief Warrant Officer 3 David L. Pearson Jr.[5] There are several warrant officer programs with differing requirements, but service as an SNCO or NCO is an important part of candidates' backgrounds.

Commissioned officers usually take a more direct route to leadership by attending college and officer training. They do not need to join the marines as privates. They can begin at a higher level through many different programs, such as Officer Candidate School. Enlisted marines who are strong leaders can find their way into the officer ranks through the Enlisted Commissioning Program. This program allows them to earn a four-year degree as they prepare for higher marine responsibilities. People hoping to become commissioned officers must be American citizens, rather than simply legal residents.

Many advantages come with rank. Starting higher up comes with benefits such as higher pay and better military housing. Marines in the higher ranks are more likely to get their choice of assignments, too. The higher a marine is in the chain of command, the more decisions he or she can make. However, higher-ranking personnel have much more responsibility than those in the lower ranks. Decisions that turn out badly come back to the officers who made them. And officers are generally expected to work more hours than lower-ranking personnel.

Like all military members, marines earn a regular paycheck based on rank. Housing is provided, or if not, the marine receives a housing and food allowance. Marines also have access to retirement plans, low-cost life insurance, money to help pay for education, and medical care that also applies to their families. Hazardous duty pay and skill-based pay are among the many bonuses the US military offers.

LIFE IN THE MARINES

Because amphibious operations are central to the marines, most marine corps bases are close to the sea. Many compare marine base living to living on a college campus, especially for those in the lower ranks. Marines will usually share a room with other marines, just as college students might share a dorm room. Higher-ranked marines can have private rooms or might live with their families in houses on or off the base.

Even when marines are confined to living on a base, that base may have all the conveniences of a town or city. Camp Pendleton, not far from San Diego, California, for example, takes up 125,000 acres (50,600 hectares) and is the workplace for many thousands of people. Its 38,000 residents have multiple

US MARINE CORPS RANKS

ENLISTED MARINES

Private
Private First Class
Lance Corporal

NONCOMMISSIONED OFFICERS (ENLISTED)

Corporal
Sergeant
Staff Sergeant
Gunnery Sergeant
Master Sergeant
First Sergeant
Master Gunnery Sergeant
Sergeant Major
Sergeant Major of the Marine Corps

WARRANT OFFICERS

Warrant Officer 1
Chief Warrant Officer 2
Chief Warrant Officer 3
Chief Warrant Officer 4
Chief Warrant Officer 5

COMMISSIONED OFFICERS

Second Lieutenant
First Lieutenant
Captain
Major
Lieutenant Colonel
Colonel
Brigadier General
Major General
Lieutenant General
General

Marines play basketball for fun at Camp Johnson in North Carolina. ★

theaters, restaurants, fitness centers, and stores, all on base. However, enjoying the luxuries of a base is not a marine's purpose. "Most of our time is spent either on deployments or in training," Sergeant Jon Davis explains. "When we aren't in one of these two situations, we are constantly being reminded that we will be soon."[6]

WELCOME TO BASIC

TO THE CRUCIBLE

Marine corps basic training turns young recruits, many fresh out of high school, into US marines in 13 weeks. The marine corps boot camp is mentally and physically grueling. That's OK, says Private First Class Brooke L. Jalbert, because "nothing is gained in the comfort zone. To be great, you have to be comfortable being uncomfortable."[7]

The training has four phases. Phase One is largely introductory; recruits learn marine corps values and history, martial arts, first aid, and how to care for uniforms and weapons. They undergo health exams and strength tests, and they begin hard physical training. Phase Two focuses on combat and marksmanship skills. Recruits also experience tear gas and learn to use a chemical protection mask.

During Phase Three, recruits face their ultimate test, a simulation called the Crucible. During these 54 hours under combat-like conditions, with little sleep or food, recruits work in teams battling each other and solving physically demanding problems they might encounter in war.

When they finish this test, recruits are considered marines. There is a Phase Four of basic training that helps marines get used to their new status. During this phase, the new marines continue physical training, taking on more responsibility for their own fitness and understanding their serious new role as defenders of the nation. As they prepare to move into their specific marine corps careers, they are finally able to talk with their instructors as fellow marines.

★ A marksmanship instructor helps a US Marine Corps recruit during training.

CHAPTER 4

SCOUT SNIPER

The mission was to take control of Baghdad, Iraq. The marines battled with machine guns and missiles, but terrorist fighters held their battalion back with a steady stream of fire. The marines couldn't seem to get control of the situation. They couldn't move forward, but they weren't about to retreat. So, the commander decided on a new tactic. He called in the sniper team.

Marine snipers may work in teams of two.

Although the marine corps is filled with skilled shooters, marine scout snipers are the experts, the best of the best. As snipers, they shoot from hidden positions to protect US troops, their allies, and sometimes civilians who find themselves in a bad place. Marine snipers do their best to live by their motto, One Shot, One Kill. That day in Baghdad, a half an hour after the commander called them, the marine scout snipers spotted and killed the seven enemy fighters who were firing on the marine battalion. This allowed the battalion to safely roll on into the city.

Scout snipers can be vital to an operation's success. Sergeant Brandon Choo, a sniper turned sniper instructor, points out snipers' effect on the enemy: "A sniper can greatly degrade the enemy's will to fight as their personnel are killed with precision direct fires."[1]

NO GLORY

Lena Sisco, a former navy intelligence officer and author of the book *Marine Scout Snipers*, observes that although marine snipers help protect their fellow marines, their lives "are not lives of glory and fame; their lives are filled with sacrifices and hardships for which they are most often not even thanked or recognized."[2] They work mostly in isolation from others. Because they may spend hours stalking and then killing an enemy soldier, they gain a reputation for cold-bloodedness, yet their actions have contributed to protecting the lives of many Americans and their allies.

On top of that, the working conditions are rough. "As a scout sniper," Choo says, "we are going to be constantly tired, fatigued, dehydrated, probably cold, for sure wet, and always hungry." The key to surviving that, he continues, is to "embrace it."[3]

TRAINING

Those who volunteer to become snipers must be extremely physically fit, highly intelligent, and expert riflemen, able to hit

★ Marine scout snipers may work from helicopters.

targets with precision rifle fire while hidden. Applicants must also have good mental health, be free of drug and alcohol abuse, have excellent eyesight (glasses are OK), and have good character. New marines cannot be scout snipers; they must have at least a rank of lance corporal. Marines who qualify for the position are first assigned to a battalion that includes scout sniper platoons. Then they can move on to training at one of several scout sniper schools, which work at making them even better.

Interest in marine sniper training has decreased, leading to a shortage of snipers. In 2017, less than half the usual number enrolled in the program, from 100 down to 42. Graduation rates also fell by more than half. From 2013 to 2018, only 226 marines graduated from scout sniper training. While once there were usually about 300 active snipers, by 2018, the number had dropped to 150.[4] Part of that declining number is due to the scout snipers achieving higher ranks and moving on to other assignments, but the number of volunteers who don't pass the course concerns marine corps leaders.

Marine leaders feel the poor graduation rate is due to marines having trouble demonstrating the stalking, marksmanship, and land navigation abilities needed to become snipers. The marine corps is experimenting with breaking the 79-day sniper training into two sections. In between, scout snipers would mentor the sniper candidates in the field. The standards for completing training would not change. "The advanced decision-making, infantry, and marksmanship skills necessary to attain this qualification make the marine Scout Sniper Course

WOMEN MOVING UP

The marine corps announced that a female lieutenant completed the Scout Sniper Unit Leaders Course in the summer of 2018. Although the three-week course is not as demanding as the longer Scout Sniper course, it prepares graduates to become sniper platoon commanders. Marines in this position decide on courses of action for scout sniper teams and direct their actions. This lieutenant, whom the marine corps did not publicly name, was the second woman to graduate from an infantry officer course.

★ A sniper demonstrates his ghillie suit.

one of the most challenging schools in the marine corps," said Captain Karoline Foote, a marine spokesperson.[5]

One of the first tasks for students in the sniper training course is to create their own camouflage, called ghillie suits. They gather up a mass of plants to drape over their heads and shoulders and then go into a stagnant pond of water. The stirred-up, mucky pond bottom takes the sheen off of the plants. Next, the soggy marines lie in the dirt to work more camouflage into their suits. The sniper students look like swamp creatures when they're done, and that's a good thing. Their lives will depend on not being spotted as they shoot from a battle hideout.

★ Marines practice with targets in shooting ranges.

Accurate shooting is essential to being a sniper. Snipers must be able to shoot targets nearly a mile away. Between shots they may have to run from station to station in full battle gear, then set up again, all without a moment to catch their breath. Sometimes, the sniper will have to calculate whether the bullet will reach a moving target based on the wind, air quality, and the Earth's curve. During training, a marine must hit 28 out of 35 shots to qualify as a sniper.

The next section of the sniper course is stalking training. By this time, the sniper candidates' matted and dusty ghillie suits are ready. Stalking, or being able to sneak up on a target without being seen, is another essential skill. The snipers have three hours to crawl through a few hundred yards of brush while instructors peer through binoculars, trying to spot them. If something looks amiss, such as a tree or bush moving with no wind, the instructors send out a person called a walker. By radio, the instructors direct the walker to where they believe the sniper is hiding. The walker moves only according to this direction, without actively seeking out the sniper. If the instructor is able to move the walker to the sniper, the marine has failed the test.

Passing the stalking test doesn't mean simply hiding well, though. When the stalkers are close to the target, it's time to shoot. After they do, instructors try again to find the stalker. If they don't, the stalker fires again. The instructor then holds up a card with large letters. Being close enough to read it means success.

Other exercises in the sniper training course increase candidates' ability to shoot from moving perches such as helicopters and at targets bobbing in the ocean. Sniper candidates also learn to shoot targets widely varying in distance, hike and run for hours on end, and rescue wounded

ONE DETERMINED MARINE

Staff Sergeant Jason Pacheco enlisted in the marines immediately after high school and, in time, completed scout sniper training. He didn't hesitate to go to difficult areas of the world and use his skills. But while deployed to Afghanistan, he stepped on an improvised explosive device (IED). These bombs, often buried along roadsides by guerrilla fighters, can kill a person or disable a military vehicle, such as a tank. This one took Pacheco's right leg. As he was being airlifted out, Pacheco told his fellow marines he'd be back. Fifteen months later, after recovering from his injury and learning to walk with a prosthetic leg, he returned to the battlefield. Pacheco was the first marine amputee who went back into combat in a specialty job.

comrades. Those left standing at the end of the grueling course are graduates.

TODAY'S BATTLES

As Sergeant Choo reports, shooting makes up only 10 percent of a marine sniper's job.[6] Scout snipers may spend days watching the battlefield. They gather information that is passed on to commanders to help with planning. Scout Sniper Logan Stutte says, "We are the eyes and the ears of the battalion. They tell me that they always are glad to hear when my team is up in the hills being their 'guardian angel.'"[7]

Fighting within cities has become common in the Middle East conflicts. While scout snipers are also experts in moving undetected within a city, the marines are at a disadvantage. Enemy fighters know their way around rows of attached houses with holes cut through the walls and other hiding places, so they know where marines might hide. The marines, however, may not know enemy snipers' hideouts. In addition, the enemy can talk to locals, even children, to figure out where marines are holed up.

This disadvantage cost the marines dearly in 2004 in Ramadi, Iraq, when Iraqi rebels discovered a team of four scout snipers. The marines were apparently surprised and never had a chance to fire before being killed. A year later, a team of six snipers was killed by rebels in Haditha, Iraq. Marine commanders are sometimes reluctant to send out snipers in pairs, thinking there is safety in larger numbers, but snipers have argued for teams of only two, saying they are less likely to be seen. The sniper team leader, Sergeant Joseph W. Chamblin, considered the deaths simply the cost of war. "It's sad they got killed," he said, "but . . .

MAKING AN IMPACT

Researcher Alexander Mello studied the battle in 2016 and 2017 to free Mosul, Iraq, from terrorism. He observed that one or two terrorist snipers may hold up a group of Iraqi fighters trying to free their city of terrorists. While one response would be to drop bombs to attack the snipers, destroying part of the city as well as possibly taking innocent lives, Mello's research showed a potentially less destructive choice would be to have scout snipers target the enemy snipers. With targeted strikes, snipers can have the same effect as a larger force of marines or larger weapons.

we've been here three years . . . and we've only had two teams killed. That's not that dramatic."[8]

AFTER THE BATTLES

In any branch of the military, those in battle must decide how they feel about their service when the battles are finished. Some can never settle their minds after seeing traumatic scenes of war and remembering the people they killed. Many military veterans suffer from post-traumatic stress disorder (PTSD) and must seek psychological treatment as they readjust to life at home.

For Sergeant Choo, the marine snipers' violent work seems a matter of simple numbers and loyalty. "I can train these marines to kill the enemy . . . and if he kills him, then other marines will live," Choo says.[9]

TOP FIVE QUESTIONS

★ HOW CAN SOMEONE PREPARE FOR THE PHYSICAL FITNESS REQUIREMENTS OF THE SCOUT SNIPER JOB?

As in all marine corps jobs, excellent physical fitness is a must for scout snipers, since they have to pass the US Marine Corps physical fitness and combat fitness tests. Before that, they must pass an Initial Strength Test to go to boot camp. People interested in becoming scout snipers should work to increase their ability to do push-ups, pull-ups, crunches, and other exercises to build strength and endurance.

★ WHAT PERSONAL SKILLS ARE USEFUL FOR SCOUT SNIPERS?

Maturity, determination, and patience are among the qualities scout snipers need. Setting goals and working hard to achieve them despite obstacles helps. When met with failure, determination means figuring out what went wrong and trying again. Solving emotional issues in positive ways is also important.

★ WHERE DO MARINE SCOUT SNIPERS WORK?

Marine scout snipers are deployed to combat areas overseas.

★ ARE THERE OTHER JOBS FOR MARINES SIMILAR TO THE SCOUT SNIPER JOB?

Reconnaissance marines are also trained as snipers. However, recon marines work on larger missions as part of special operations, meaning they more often work with members of other military branches or government agencies rather than just in marine corps missions.

★ WHAT SORT OF CIVILIAN JOBS DOES THE SCOUT SNIPER FIELD PREPARE A PERSON FOR?

After leaving the marines, scout snipers can find jobs using some of their skills in law enforcement or at private security firms. Aside from that, the discipline and determination marines develop in this position are useful in many jobs.

CHAPTER 5

COUNTERINTELLIGENCE/HUMAN INTELLIGENCE SPECIALIST

The marine corps' counterintelligence/human intelligence (CI/HUMINT) specialists are tasked with collecting information that can help identify and stop enemy spies and terrorists. They need to be able to gather information from citizens in countries where marines are deployed. They also need to question prisoners.

Marines on human intelligence missions connect with local people and military soldiers in other countries.

The work of CI/HUMINT specialists is secretive, so these marines are not often seen in uniform. They dress casually to keep a low profile. Since they usually don't display their rank and share their full identity, their hard work is often not recognized or praised.

The marine corps frequently calls for qualified marines to move into this career, citing a shortage of CI/HUMINT specialists. In 2019, the marine corps offered a $90,000 bonus for those willing to make the move and commit to six years

WHY THE SHORTAGE?

Most careers in the marine corps involve at least some stressful or even hazardous work, and many positions involve additional training. So what causes so many openings in the CI/HUMINT job? For some, work runs around the clock, as people in this job never know when a chance to get valuable information might arise. Eating, sleeping, and free time must give way to the demands of the job. Specialists may be alone in remote areas for long stretches. Contacting family is often not a possibility for months without endangering themselves and others.

in the job. The marine corps offers this not only because of the constant need for marines in this career but also because the position involves stressful, hazardous work requiring extensive training.

REQUIREMENTS

Personal characteristics are important for CI/HUMINT specialists. "Outstanding communication skills which enable them to interact with a wide variety of people under any circumstance" are required, states the 2019 call for applicants, adding that "intellect, flexibility, creativity, and diverse cultural experience are invaluable traits."[1] Being a self-starting hard worker who feels rewarded simply for doing the job well helps too.

CI/HUMINT specialists need a top secret security clearance. Applicants must be at least 21, have a solid record of service in the marines, and a rank between corporal and sergeant.

They also take a polygraph test and undergo a long interview. Clear, descriptive writing ability is also essential, as national security may depend on the specialist's skill in reporting on the people, places, and information he or she learns about. That means the specialist must have good typing skills as well.

SECURITY CLEARANCES

Certain government and military jobs require security clearances to access classified information. The top secret security clearance required for CI/HUMINT specialists is the most restrictive. The first test for someone seeking a security clearance is completing a thorough background check. Investigators consider legal troubles, large debt and lack of responsibility in addressing it, drug use, and the likelihood of foreign influence, among other things.

TRAINING

Once a CI/HUMINT applicant is approved, training begins. It can take up to two years. The first step is Pre-Resident Training (PRT). PRT introduces marines to the skills and knowledge they will need to acquire to become CI/HUMINT specialists. From there, it's on to Virginia Beach, Virginia, and the Marine Corps Intelligence Schools. There, the applicant takes the Marine Air Ground Task Force CI/HUMINT Course. This intense 91-day training introduces candidates to the supportive role CI/HUMINT specialists play for the rest of the marine corps. It educates the candidates on procedures and methods for gathering intelligence. The specialists need to understand the workings of the coordinated teams of marine

★ The work of CI/HUMINT specialists supports other marines, including those in combat.

air- and ground-combat units as they are often called upon to provide intelligence.

While they sometimes work with partners or small teams, CI/HUMINT specialists often work alone. This means they need to think for themselves and act without immediate approval from a superior. This aspect of the training course—and the job—is especially challenging for some marines, who were taught as recruits to always follow orders.

Good intuition and follow-through help marines complete the CI/HUMINT training course. “The majority of the school is not academic, it’s performance-based,” a CI/HUMINT master sergeant explains in *Military Times*. (Like most people working in the intelligence community, he does not want to be named publicly for confidentiality reasons.) “You’re put into scenarios,” he continues, “and dealing with role players playing different types of people in those scenarios. There's often a lot of ambiguity when you're dealing with personalities and . . . the way people think and act. It's not a science."[2] Most CI/HUMINT specialists follow the training course with a year of intensive training in a foreign language to equip them for working overseas.

ON THE JOB

The master sergeant recalled that, as a marine in the infantry, he always understood that the job before him was to find the enemy, get close to them, and eliminate them. However, he discovered that the CI/HUMINT specialist's job was much more complex in the ways that gathering intelligence supports combat marines. "I had no idea what went into finding the enemy . . . in the first place. [Even] if it's some type of peacekeeping mission

MAKING AN IMPACT

The observations and analysis of counterintelligence/human intelligence specialists are vital in military decision-making and can influence whether battles are fought. The work of enlisted CI/HUMINT specialists influences the decisions of those in ranks well above their own, an unusual occurrence in the military. CI/HUMINT specialists are often not recognized for their discoveries and analyses that save lives. Their work affects not only battlefields and war-torn communities but also the United States, as they may uncover plots against the country.

or something that doesn't involve direct combat, there's so much that goes on behind the scenes so that the infantry and other forces can go out and actually do their missions."[3]

One common task for CI/HUMINT specialists is to develop friendly relationships with local villagers. Often villagers have contact with terrorists and may have vital information. The specialists will have to win the trust of reluctant informants who are often of a different culture. Cultural differences can make this a challenge. In many cases, male CI/HUMINT specialists have been cut off from communicating with female villagers because, in some societies, women don't freely speak with men who aren't their relatives.

CI/HUMINT specialists are a part of the marine corps' Special Operations Forces, so they may often work with other branches of the military. While specialists often travel with the infantry, some work with US embassy staff. Others are assigned to allies' military forces and even their police forces. Some specialists remain in the United States, working to analyze weaknesses in US military facilities and designing ways to eliminate them. They also work to protect information and procedures that might be useful to enemies. Some marine CI/HUMINT specialists are assigned to US government agencies such as the Federal Bureau of Investigation (FBI), the Central Intelligence Agency (CIA), and the Department of Homeland Security.

TOP FIVE QUESTIONS

★ WHAT HIGH SCHOOL CLASSES WOULD BE HELPFUL TO SOMEONE PLANNING TO GO INTO COUNTERINTELLIGENCE/HUMAN INTELLIGENCE?

Any classes in foreign languages, cultural and religious studies, psychology, and writing would be helpful.

★ WHAT PERSONAL SKILLS ARE HELPFUL FOR CI/HUMINT SPECIALISTS?

CI/HUMINT specialists must have great communication and critical-thinking skills. They also must be self-motivated and comfortable working alone at times.

★ WHAT HAPPENS IF A PERSON DOES NOT FINISH THE CI/HUMINT SPECIALIST TRAINING COURSE?

More than half of those who begin the CI/HUMINT course don't finish. If they have earned a higher rank during the course, they are returned to their earlier rank and given a different work assignment.

★ HOW MUCH ARE CI/HUMINT SPECIALISTS PAID?

Since marines need to be at least at the rank of corporal to apply for this job, pay would generally start at about $2,194 to $2,664 monthly, apart from bonuses.[4] Additional time in service and additional training bring more pay.

★ WHICH CIVILIAN JOBS DOES WORKING AS A MARINE CI/HUMINT SPECIALIST PREPARE A PERSON FOR?

Having top-security clearance is valuable in many government jobs, as is the ability to analyze information. Private security, personal security, and background investigation all call upon skills learned in CI/HUMINT training. Those who have learned a foreign language can also work as translators, interpreters, and teachers.

CHAPTER 6

COMBAT PHOTOGRAPHER

Tammy Hineline started out shooting baby pictures at Walmart. Community college just wasn't capturing her imagination, except perhaps the photography classes. On a whim, she signed on with the marines. Six years later, she was a marine sergeant and a photographer. As a marine, she has

Marine photographers may use different lenses and other specific camera equipment to capture photos amid combat.

done two deployments, traveled to seven countries, and taken many photos.

The job of combat photographers is to take pictures during combat. Their main purpose is to support the marines' mission. These pictures will have historical significance, but they can also be useful in planning battle strategies and in keeping the public informed. Combat photographers are also called upon to photograph ceremonies, training, and other events.

★ A combat photographer checks her camera while working on a helicopter during a training mission.

GETTING STARTED

Although she works as a photographer, "we are marines first," Hineline says.[1] That means going through boot camp, keeping up rifle skills, and staying physically fit. The motto "Every marine a rifleman" applies to those who shoot pictures as well. Once boot camp is complete, privates through staff sergeants can apply to become photographers. They need to score well on a technical exam and have normal color vision and US citizenship. Since their work may involve sensitive pictures and information, a secret security clearance is also required. Those who have abused drugs or alcohol in the past or who have committed crimes may be turned away.

Once accepted, marines attend a still photography course at Fort Meade, Maryland, along with photographers-to-be from the other military branches. There they'll learn the basics of operating and maintaining a digital camera, working with light, transmitting and archiving images, and communicating Department of Defense themes. By demonstrating previously acquired photography skills, some may be excused from part of the course.

OTHER COMBAT CAMERA JOBS

Some marines, like Hineline, choose to get training in more than one related field. Hineline is also a combat videographer. This job is much the same as the photographer job except that it involves filming video instead. An effective videographer imagines the story the video will tell, writes the script, and edits out sections that don't support the story. Special effects and audio enhance the video. Their videos are used for everything from public viewing to training to battlefield information. Another job, combat camera production, is focused on preparing the final product. Rather than being in combat, marines in this job come up with ideas for visuals to be used for a variety of purposes and in many different formats. Their work includes designing web pages and operating special equipment and software.

TAKING PICTURES

A combat photographer's work includes photographing day or night, in rain or sun, and even underwater. The types of photographs also depend on the unit to which the photographer is assigned. For example, Hineline says, "If you're with a Headquarters Squadron you'll mostly be doing promotion photos, administrative things,

VIDEOGRAPHER EARNS VALOR AWARD

Twenty-one-year-old Corporal Neill A. Sevelius, a videographer, is one example of a marine bravely saving another. His squad of marines had been taking fire all day as it tried to move into a boarded-up house. Another squad was on a roof. When Sevelius saw a marine fall, he rushed to help, discovering the other marine had a deep but non–life-threatening wound. Sevelius helped him get off the roof and to additional help. After receiving a marine award for valor in relation to that incident, Sevelius said, "Marines do great stuff every day, I just happened to get noticed."[5]

and ceremonies."[2] She describes photographing training exercises as a fun part of the job. She enjoyed capturing images of a humanitarian effort to rescue civilians in Tunisia, too.

However, going to the battlefield with the troops, says Hineline, is "the peak" of a combat photographer's career, though it can be "very difficult physically and emotionally."[3] Photographer Reece Lodder, who, like Hineline, captured shots of marines fighting in Afghanistan, points to the significance of the work: "My goal was to bridge that gap between what you can see and what you can't see . . . to tell what the moment is like."[4]

Peak experience or not, the battlefield is a dangerous place to be. And combat photographers are not there as extras, people to be shoved to safety. They carry rifles and are expected to let go of their cameras and use their rifles when needed. Many combat photographers have been wounded or killed while fighting or photographing battles. Even during training or on humanitarian efforts, there is sometimes loss of life.

Like others in combat, photographers may suffer from PTSD. Often, the pictures they must take are disturbing. Navy Commander Thomas Cotton of the Fort Meade Joint Combat Camera Center for Defense Media Activity says the photographer may have "to go over the photographs . . . and relive it over and over. The incident is done, and you are still dealing with it."[6]

The photographer's job is extremely demanding in other ways, too. Hineline recalls working 12 hours every day except for half

MAKING AN IMPACT

Photos of battles can give the public a clearer feel for what is happening during military conflict. This can be important to family of service members and voters concerned about military actions. Photos can also influence people considering enlisting. For example, boot camp photos give a good sense of what recruits should expect.

The photographer's work has other vital roles as well. Combat photographers often take pictures of landscapes so that the marines can picture the battle. They will know in advance whether there are obstructions, such as waterways or difficult terrain. Pictures taken following the battle can help them reflect on how well things went. Both sorts of pictures can be helpful to commanders in deciding on troop action. Photographs can also provide evidence in investigations.

A combat photographer shoots photos from aboard an amphibious assault ship.

days on Friday and Sunday. There's no bell signaling the end of a shift, though. If the action continues past 12 hours, so does the photographer. "But that's how it is . . . for everyone," says Hineline. "The war doesn't stop on weekends or evenings."[7]

Still, Hineline says she feels good about her marine photography career. She's had experiences with people and places she wouldn't have otherwise. She's learned to work quickly in stressful situations, and she's been able to improve her skills in photography, which she enjoys. She also has a portfolio full of photos she can use to shift into a civilian photography career if she chooses to do so.

TOP FIVE QUESTIONS

★ HOW CAN A STUDENT PREPARE FOR A CAREER IN COMBAT PHOTOGRAPHY?

Taking photography courses can naturally put a student ahead of the curve. But even if a photography course is not available, students can prepare by taking and analyzing digital pictures. Practice taking photos in varied situations will be most helpful. This includes photographing both action and still subjects from different distances and in varied lighting conditions.

★ WHAT TESTS ARE REQUIRED TO QUALIFY FOR THE COMBAT PHOTOGRAPHER JOB?

Along with the standard requirements for enlisting in the military, combat photographers must earn a score of at least 100 on the general technical part of the ASVAB test.

★ HOW LONG DOES COMBAT PHOTOGRAPHER TRAINING TAKE?

The military's basic still photography course lasts for four months. Additional photography courses, such as photojournalism and mass communication, are also available.

★ WHERE DO COMBAT PHOTOGRAPHERS WORK?

Marine combat photographers work wherever the marines are. That often means going overseas. But it also includes marine bases in the United States. While most of their work is done in the field capturing images, they also spend some time in computer labs editing photos.

★ WHICH CIVILIAN CAREERS DOES COMBAT PHOTOGRAPHY PREPARE A PERSON FOR?

Many former combat photographers open their own photography studios or work for other studios. Working as a photographer for magazines or newspapers is another possibility.

CHAPTER 7

DOG HANDLER

Kepie has an unusual but important job: he helps protect the US president. Kepie is a long-haired German shepherd and a US marine. His handler, Corporal Christopher Vogt, says, "The dogs are just as much marines as we are . . . if we go on a run, they go on a run with us."[1] Vogt and Kepie train daily to stay in shape for their duties. They are assigned to a helicopter squadron and protect all equipment related to the

Dog handlers are trained to work closely with their dogs as a team.

president's travel. The squadron has six of the approximately 2,300 military dogs in the US military.[2] Kepie's specialty is detecting explosives. German shepherds and Belgian Malinois are two of the most common breeds to become military working dogs. They are powerful and intelligent, with excellent senses of smell.

MILITARY POLICE

Marines hoping for the much-desired dog handler career must first become military police (MP) officers. After completing

Marine Combat Training, marines from private to master gunnery sergeant can apply for MP training. They must meet many requirements. They must be at least 19 years old when the training is completed, be eligible for a secret security clearance, and be in good physical condition and at least 65 inches (165 cm) tall. They also must have clear speech, normal color vision, and US citizenship. They can have no history of mental, emotional, or nervous disorders, nor can they have committed crimes or have other evidence of poor behavior. Finally, applicants must score well on required tests.

Once marines complete MP training, they can immediately apply for the working dog basic handler course. Despite the applicants having qualified for and completed MP training, officials carefully choose which marines become dog handlers. The competition is tough, and the marine corps wants to be sure the best people are matched with the dogs. Applicants' previous

MILITARY WORKING DOGS' JOURNEY

Many military dogs are bred and born in Europe. Others come from the same place they'll be trained, Lackland Air Force Base in Texas. All get the title of military working dog (MWD). Their names indicate where they're from. A double consonant at the start means they're from Lackland, so a Lackland pup might be called MWD Rrex. Dogs graduate from their training in 120 days. Then they are sent to a base. Most will be assigned one handler; some will work with multiple handlers. Dogs average about eight years in the military before retiring. Many are then adopted by their handlers as pets.

★ Marine dog handlers must learn how to take care of military working dogs.

records will be studied again, including classwork, exams, and even conduct and activities, before they become marines. Senior instructors interview the candidates on their knowledge of the marine corps and ask personal questions. Candidates may have to write an essay explaining why they want to become dog handlers. Sometimes, the marines stage contests in which candidates compete in answering questions about the marine corps and their job. The reason for all this competition is simply that the dog handler job is very popular. “If you want to be an MP, do all you can to get into the canine community,” says dog handler Corporal Braxton H. Rico. “Stick out amongst everyone else.”[3]

After a dog handler candidate is selected, he or she starts with basic training for the job, including how to feed dogs and keep kennels clean, along with getting familiar with equipment and relating effectively to the dogs. This training can last for as long as six months before the handler begins the Department of Defense’s Military Working Dog Program, or “Dog School.” All branches of the military send their handler candidates to Lackland Air Force Base for this course. Before working with dogs, candidates learn dog care, training methods, and psychology.

Military dog handlers must understand how a dog’s mind works. This is essential for handlers’ ability to train and care for their canine partners. Handlers also need to watch for signs of stress and PTSD in their dogs. About 5 percent of dogs in battle will be affected; some, after veterinary treatment, can return to battle.[4] Making sure the dogs get rest during training and at work can reduce stress.

The dogs are also preparing for their roles. As puppies, they learn to relate to people in foster homes. Those that show promise as military working dogs begin training between the ages of 18 and 24 months. To some extent, the best training method for a dog depends on its personality. There is an effort

★ Handlers may run their dogs through obstacle courses for training.

to match the personality of the handler to the dog, too. The pair needs to be a good fit as the two will have a close working relationship. As handlers feed, bathe, and exercise their dogs, the handlers and dogs build a strong bond. "By no means is this job easy," says Sergeant Shawn R. Edens. "You're in charge of this dog who basically has a mind of a three-year-old, so you're constantly keeping an eye on him while ensuring you take care of him."[5]

Handlers wear protective gear for teaching dogs how to bite and attack. 

In addition to teaching basic commands to their dogs, handlers work to strengthen their dogs' bite to hold on when ordered to attack a person. Handlers wear an arm covering to prevent injury during this training. The dog must hold on to the handler's covered arm until told to release. Scented rubber toys are used to teach the dog to search. Handlers rehearse situations they may face in the field with their dogs. Dogs also need to get used to different travel experiences, including the loud noises of aircraft during takeoffs and landings.

Marine corps dogs may learn to patrol, scout, search buildings, or find drugs or explosives. While many dogs work on long leashes, specialized search dogs are trained to work off leash to find improvised explosive devices (IEDs), bomb-making materials, ammunition, and other threats. The dogs figure out search patterns for themselves and are remarkably good at focusing on areas where dangerous material is most likely to be hidden. They can even find buried materials. Being off leash gives dogs much more flexibility and keeps their handlers farther from the danger.

During training, handlers take careful notes on how each dog was trained, how well the dog did, and what needs more work. Training continues long after the course has formally ended. Upon completing the course, handlers take a test to become certified. They need to show that they can give appropriate

A PURPLE HEART FOR YEAGER

Sergeant Yeager, a Labrador retriever, went on more than 100 combat patrols during his service in Iraq and Afghanistan. On one mission in Afghanistan, an IED exploded, killing Yeager's handler, Lance Corporal Abraham Tarwoe. Yeager and Tarwoe were attempting to clear the way for a marine battalion when the IED went off. Yeager lost part of an ear in the explosion and developed bladder problems and PTSD. Yeager returned to the United States, where he was treated and then retired in an adopted home. The mission earned him a Purple Heart award, a high honor in the military for those killed or wounded in the line of duty.

commands and understand the dog's responses. Handlers and dogs recertify yearly.

ON THE JOB

After the course, handlers are assigned to their specific dogs. The handlers and dogs then have a month to build a bond. Vogt explains, "You walk with them; you play with them. That dog needs to learn you. He needs to trust everything you say, so he needs to be able to know your voice and be able to know what you do and how you're going to react."[6]

Dog handlers work in many settings. For example, every marine base has its own canine unit. The teams patrol the base and do sweeps, or searches. "Each dog is [trained for] either explosives or narcotics, so the dog is in tune with its objective," says Sergeant Todd W. Shires, the kennel master at the US Marine Corps Recruit Depot, San Diego. "They are all trained for 100 percent accuracy."[7]

A dog's sense of smell can be up to 100,000 times stronger than people's.[8] If dogs start to misidentify their targets, they will be retrained and recertified. The dogs on the San Diego marine corps base are rotated among the handlers, so both handlers and dogs are used to working with various partners. Sometimes the teams help at other bases, including those of other military branches, and give public demonstrations. These activities help the dogs deal with different settings.

In battle, dog handlers have a lot to manage. "Not only do I have to handle and pay attention to my dog and read his behavior while I'm working him," says handler Corporal Jesica Fleming, "I also have a full kit [battle gear] and rifle. I'm looking for visual indicators of IEDs or any possible threats. It's a lot

MAKING AN IMPACT

"It's estimated that each military dog saves the lives of 150 to 200 servicemen and women," reports Robin Ganzert, president of American Humane, an organization that serves animals.[9] Dogs and their handlers often lead the way when battalions move, making sure the area is free of IEDs and other hazards. The dogs protect people in large crowds by sniffing for explosives. They capture enemy fighters and hold them for their handlers. "If I didn't have him, there were a lot of situations where people could have been hurt," says handler Corporal Anthony Brecht. Technology often fails to find explosives, he says. "There's no equipment available that will do what a dog can do. They're very instrumental."[10]

more to do at one time."[11] To dog handlers, though, it's well worth the extra effort. One reason is the companionship. "No matter what, no matter where you go, you always have somebody you know," says handler Corporal Dustin Johnson.[12] Another reason is the loyalty and trust they develop. "I'd save his life, and he'd save mine," Lance Corporal Fidel E. Rodriguez says.[13]

Marine military working dogs, like dogs in other branches, are considered members of the US military. When they receive awards, the occasion is marked with ceremony, just as military honors accompany their burials. The dogs even hold ranks. Tradition dictates that they rank one step above their handlers, a reminder that they are to be treated with respect.

TOP FIVE QUESTIONS

★ HOW CAN A STUDENT PREPARE FOR A CAREER AS A MARINE DOG HANDLER?

There are three goals to think about for this career: preparing to be a marine, preparing for MP duty, and preparing to work with dogs. Fitness and knowledge of marine corps life helps with the first goal. Participation in career-prep programs run by police, such as the Police Athletic League or Police Explorers, will help with the second. Raising and training a dog or working with an organization that does this offers experience for the third goal. Reading about these subjects is another way to learn.

★ ARE THERE ANY SPECIAL PHYSICAL REQUIREMENTS FOR A DOG HANDLER?

Like any combat-ready marine, a handler must stay in excellent physical condition. The handler must be able to lift the dog, who usually weighs about 100 pounds (45 kg), and carry the additional gear needed for the dog along with his or her own gear.

★ HOW LONG IS A DOG HANDLER'S TRAINING?

While the handler must first take military police training and should expect to keep training a canine partner after the course ends, the Military Working Dog Program at Lackland Air Force Base is 11 weeks long.

★ HOW DO DOG HANDLERS BECOME CERTIFIED?

After training, dog and handler have to demonstrate that they understand each other. Dogs need to obey commands and handlers must be able to interpret their dogs' behavior.

★ WHICH CIVILIAN CAREERS DOES BEING A MARINE DOG HANDLER PREPARE A PERSON FOR?

Working for law enforcement on a federal, state, or local level is a natural fit for a former marine dog handler.

CHAPTER 8

AIRCRAFT MECHANIC

"It was exciting!" Dustin Gulley says about his first day with the US Marine Corps Hornet Squadron. "And the sense of pride was overwhelming," he added.[1] The new aircraft mechanic was a lance corporal and just 18 years old. The Hornet—the F/A-18 Hornet aircraft, that is—has been used by the military since the early 1980s. Carrying up to 17,000 pounds (7,700 kg) of ammunition, the Hornet gets its jobs done.

An aircraft mechanic works on a CH-53E Super Stallion helicopter.

Although his job title was mechanic, Gulley didn't do much repair work at first. "I spent most of my first couple of months playing gopher for the other guys while trying to pick up on as much knowledge as I possibly could," he explains. "I took every opportunity to get one-on-one instruction with the other guys, and I feel like they respected me for that."[2] He discovered that the marine corps' mechanic training only went so far. Learning on the job was important, too. Soon, Gulley was servicing struts and checking out hydraulic systems with the rest of the squadron. Later, he became the youngest team member testing a new fighter plane, the F-35 Lightning II.

BECOMING AN AIRCRAFT MECHANIC

Marines seeking aircraft mechanic jobs begin working in aircraft maintenance. They can begin immediately after boot camp at the rank of private first class. These jobs involve routine upkeep of aircraft. From there, marines can learn to maintain and repair various airplane or helicopter parts and may eventually work up to manager or supervisory roles.

Corporal James Ganieany became a helicopter airframe mechanic within a year after graduating from high school. Four years later, he was teaching younger mechanics to work with

AIRCRAFT MAINTAINERS

Closely connected to the marines' aircraft mechanics, aircraft maintainers take care of the routine work that keeps aircraft sailing smoothly through the sky. Lance Corporal Tyler Ngiraswei compares them to a race car's pit crew. They carefully go over the aircraft to spot any problems, resolve them, and top off the fuel tanks. "We literally cannot fly without the maintenance marines," states pilot Captain Nils P. Alpers. "Without the maintainers, the aircraft would not get fixed, fueled and would not be able to taxi, let alone take off."[3] They are also the first line of protection for pilot and crew. They see the aircraft coming and going. When an aircraft lands, a maintainer guides it to its parking spot. With the engine still running, the pilot and maintainer check all the systems. The systems are checked again before flights.

Aircraft mechanics work with other marines including other mechanics and aircraft maintainers.

CH-53E Super Stallion helicopters. His work sent him to the Pacific Ocean several times. Wherever aircraft land, the marines may need mechanics.

BECOMING A PILOT

Marines interested in aviation can also pursue the job of pilot. Since all pilots are officers, the first step toward this career is getting a bachelor's degree. Officer training comes next, followed by six weeks to build the basic knowledge pilots must have. This includes an understanding of airplanes, how they fly, navigation, and survival tactics on both land and sea. Many hours go into primary flight training both in the air and in flight simulators. After this is completed, the pilot candidate is picked to fly a particular type of aircraft, such as jets or helicopters. The aircraft type determines the length and location of intermediate and advanced training. Those who progress this far earn their wings as marine corps pilots.

Gulley put little thought into his career choice. In fact, he can't say why he requested the aircraft mechanic job. As a child, he had focused on computers. He hadn't done much with vehicle repairs before the marines "except to do oil changes and the occasional brake job," he says. But he adds that working on aircraft seemed "cool."[4] After boot camp, Gulley was sent to the Naval Air Technical Training Center in Pensacola, Florida, to learn to be an airframer. This title allows a marine to work on all parts of an aircraft except propellers, engines, and the dials and gauges in the cockpit. These specialties fall to other mechanics. Like other students, he had to pass written, verbal, and practical exams, demonstrating skills on a disabled aircraft.

ON THE JOB

Aircraft mechanics do much of their work in hangars. They also work at repair stations and on airfields. Like Ganieany, mechanics often travel to keep aircraft going overseas. If not stationed in a battle zone, they may sightsee and enjoy the area while they are not working.

Work shifts of 12 or more hours are not uncommon for aircraft mechanics. Sometimes mechanics are pushed to work quickly to ready planes for missions. And yet, the safety and reliability of the aircraft need to always be in the forefront of mechanics' minds as they work. Aircraft mechanics may also struggle with shortages of supplies they need. Ordered parts might not arrive for a week, and then they might be the wrong parts or broken. Repairs are frequent because of aircraft age and overuse.

MAKING AN IMPACT

Aircraft mechanics are needed to keep the marine corps' aircraft capable of flying. Keeping pilots in the air isn't just important for combat missions. When pilots aren't flying often enough, they aren't practicing their skills. Lack of practice leads to pilot error, which can cause aircraft crashes. Of course, mechanical problems can also cause crashes. Mechanics evaluate each aircraft and its parts to make sure it is safe and flight ready. They keep aircraft in the air so pilots can practice, assist in humanitarian efforts, and go to battle.

However, the marine corps has been upgrading its fleet. In 2018, the marines' deputy commandant for aviation, Lieutenant General Steven R. Rudder, set several goals. The first was to be combat ready. The second was to update the corps' aircraft and to ensure speedy maintenance and repair of aircraft. Marines like Gulley and Ganieany will be instrumental in achieving these goals.

TOP FIVE QUESTIONS

★ HOW CAN A STUDENT PREPARE FOR A CAREER AS AN AIRCRAFT MECHANIC?

Since mechanics use hand and power tools, opportunities to work with these will benefit a future aircraft mechanic. Learning about engine mechanics will also help. Students may also want to read about how aircraft work.

★ WHAT IS THE AVERAGE SALARY FOR AN AIRCRAFT MECHANIC?

According to *Today's Military*, in 2019, $56,000 per year was the average military salary for aircraft mechanics, though, as with all military careers, it will vary based on rank and time served.[5]

★ DO AIRCRAFT MECHANICS WORK ON UNMANNED AIRCRAFT?

No, unmanned aerial vehicle mechanic is a separate job in the marine corps. The marine corps has three active units for unmanned aircraft systems and expects to use them in many types of military missions.

★ DO AIRCRAFT MECHANICS NEED A SECURITY CLEARANCE?

Some do. It depends on which unit the mechanic is assigned to. Mechanics working on experimental aircraft or aircraft carrying secret equipment or other material will need one. Any classified projects, such as those involved with cutting-edge F-35 fighter jets, will require mechanics to have security clearance.

★ WHAT SORT OF CIVILIAN CAREERS DOES WORKING AS A MARINE AIRCRAFT MECHANIC PREPARE A PERSON FOR?

There are numerous and growing opportunities for civilians in this field. Commercial airlines need mechanics, and learning to work with various aircraft will give a former marine mechanic an advantage in this career.

CHAPTER 9

MARINE BAND MUSICIAN

The US Marine Band has been around since President John Adams created it in 1798. By 1801, the band treated him to its first concert at the White House. In those days, the band boasted a drum major and a fife major leading 32 drums and fifes. President Thomas Jefferson called the band

The US Marine Corps band known as "The President's Own" includes the branch's most elite musicians.

"The President's Own," and it hasn't missed a presidential inauguration since his. Today, the band is also the United States' oldest professional musical organization. It has a reputation for excellence that justifies its longevity.

Although marine musicians are commonly referred to as members of "the band," the marine corps actually has 12 bands. Only one is referred to as "The President's Own" now, and it has the most sought-after positions. The "Every marine a rifleman" motto aside, members of this special group of musicians are the

MAKING DRUM MAJOR HISTORY

Gunnery Sergeant Stacie Crowther wanted to learn something new. She wanted to challenge herself. And so, she made history. In the fall of 2016, she auditioned for and won the position of assistant drum major for "The President's Own." She was the first woman in the position.

Crowther stepped into her role in March 2017, leading the band in various ceremonies, taking charge of the unit, and training new members. She recalls her first time leading a marine band: "The wall of sound behind me was incredible, and I couldn't believe I was the one in front." For what she considered "an absolute honor," Crowther was awarded the Navy and Marine Corps Commendation Medal for meritorious service.[1] Less than two years later, she took on a fresh challenge as bandmaster of the Quantico (Virginia) Marine Band and a new rank, master sergeant.

only marines who do not need to participate in basic training. They enlist and head straight to Washington, DC, to practice their art.

BECOMING "THE PRESIDENT'S OWN"

Auditioning for "The President's Own" is very much like auditioning for a major symphony orchestra. Candidates perform behind a screen so the audition committee considers only their skill in playing. Those who make the cut follow up with an audition that involves playing with current band members. The committee needs to know that candidates are excellent musicians who will blend well with the band. Candidates must also go through a physical exam. While marines in this premier band don't have to go through boot camp or even pass the fitness test, they need to look the part, and they need to be in good health. Because they sometimes perform at the White House, they need to be eligible for top secret security clearance. They also need to sight-read music easily and demonstrate world-class performance skills.

Most of the musicians who qualify for the Marine Band have an impressive musical history before they sign on. Lead violinist Staff Sergeant Karen Johnson, for example, began learning music when she was four years old. She earned a bachelor's degree from the world-renowned Julliard School in New York City and a master's degree in music from the University of Maryland. She had also studied under some noted teachers. Before winning a spot in "The President's Own," she worked with

REACHING OUT

Reaching out to the public is a fun duty for marine musicians. For example, in April 2019, "The President's Own" gave a free concert for children in Alexandria, Virginia. The band played a lively mix of jazz and pop tunes. After the concert, children were able to ask the musicians questions, examine the instruments, and try to play them. "While young people will learn about the different sections in the big band, the role of the rhythm section, a variety of other musical styles, and even the concept of improvisation, they will walk away with a memory of the incredible sound, and how it makes them feel," said Conductor Assistant Director Captain Ryan J. Nowlin.[2]

Marine Band musicians play at many different types of events and ceremonies.

several state and city orchestras. Percussionist Master Sergeant David Murray began playing at age 12. Before he joined the Marine Band at age 24, he had nine years' worth of public performances, including performing with orchestras in famous places such as the Hollywood Bowl and Moscow Conservatory.

Musicians who make it through the selection process enlist for four years and begin their service as staff sergeant. With this rank, the musicians can earn a salary similar to what they would earn in civilian bands or orchestras. The special group of musicians plays with not only the Marine Band but also the Chamber Orchestra and Chamber Ensembles.

In addition to performing at the White House, the Marine Band gives concerts in and around Washington, DC. Each year, it also tours the country to perform. While "The President's Own" rarely travels beyond the United States, it gave a concert in Japan in 2019, and it performed in Switzerland in 2001. Murray says, "I was attracted to a career with 'The President's Own' because I get to play with some of the greatest musicians in the world, in a really wide range of musical styles and ensembles, and I have a front row seat for historical events."[3]

"THE COMMANDANT'S OWN" DRUM AND BUGLE CORPS

Another special unit is "The Commandant's Own" Drum and Bugle Corps. Eighty-five musicians make up this marching group. The group performs in Washington Marine Barracks and Arlington Cemetery war memorial parades as well as at almost 500 other national and overseas occasions yearly. Its annual travel takes the group more than 50,000 miles (80,000 km).[4]

Originally, drummers and buglers performed on the battlefield, sending musical instructions to the troops to fight on, withdraw, and so forth. It became an official unit in 1934, serving patriotic functions. Today's Drum and Bugle Corps often performs its unique two-instrument music at many public events. "We didn't have many people coming to band concerts," Lance Corporal Brian Bumgarner says of his earlier nonmilitary band experiences.[5] Wanting to be a marine and continue in a marching band before large crowds, he auditioned when the Drum and Bugle Corps had a bugler opening. As part of "The Commandant's Own," he says, "We go outside and perform with a marching band and get the same crowd that you have at football games."[6]

Potential marine drummers and buglers can give their first auditions before joining the marines. Afterward, a marine musician technical assistant will let them know whether being accepted is a realistic goal and how they should prepare. Usually, they're directed to get private lessons, so arranging an audition a year ahead is a good idea. But first, unlike "The President's Own," members of "The Commandant's Own" go through boot camp and infantry training. From there, those selected for the Drum and Bugle Corps begin their primary job, perfecting skills with the rest of the marine corps.

FIELD BANDS

Musicians who like a lot of variety may be best suited for one of the marine corps' ten field bands. As their recruiting website states, these musicians "perform as the full spectrum of ensembles to include wind ensemble, ceremonial band, jazz big band, pop rock band, as well as brass and woodwind chamber ensembles."[7]

MAKING AN IMPACT

Marine Band musicians aim to inspire the troops and the country to support them. Bandsman Staff Sergeant Victor Norris felt the impact of this while playing the marine hymn with the band. "A World War II veteran got out of his wheelchair and stood at attention," Norris said. "I have never felt more pride of my country." Like other Marine Band musicians, Norris is proud of what the bands represent. He said, "Around the world, we are opening doors through music for our nation, for our armed forces, and for the marine corps."[8]

“Making a career out of music is very difficult, as any music major knows,” says Warrant Officer Alex Panos, a band officer.[9] That’s one reason marine bands travel the country: they want to let high schoolers and college musicians see that joining the marines is a way to keep making music. They don’t promise an easy road there, though. The audition puts candidates through their paces: performance skill, sight-reading, and knowledge of music theory are important, as they are with the other professional bands. Like “The Commandant’s Own,” field band recruits go through boot camp and combat training. They have to keep up these skills, too, as they may be called upon to pick up a rifle. After combat training comes the Naval School of Music for six months of job-specific training. Once they’ve finished that, the marines can choose their top three field bands; the marine corps tries to honor their choices but must also consider band needs. The bands are stationed along the US East Coast and in California, Hawaii, Louisiana, and Japan.

Fitness and field training and military education, along with rehearsals, are part of the musicians’ daily routine. But plans change along with the season and performances, and the bands travel both nationally and internationally. As he wrapped up his time with the Marine Band, Staff Sergeant Mark Pellon said, “For me personally, this has been an invaluable career choice, because I know many professional musicians that wish they

★ Marine Band members represent the US Marine Corps, the US military, and the United States.

could have traveled the world playing music, that wish they had instruments provided for them, [and] a college education which I got provided to me."[10]

The US Marine Corps needs people of nearly every temperament and talent. Some sign up for the marines for just a few years to learn skills, further their education, be part of a team, test themselves, or see more of the world, and then they move on to civilian careers. Others decide to stay with the marines for 20 or more years, working their way into respected leadership positions. For many years to come, the US Marine Corps will continue to defend the nation and to provide humanitarian aid and deliver disaster relief around the world.

TOP FIVE QUESTIONS

★ HOW CAN A STUDENT PREPARE TO JOIN A MARINE BAND?

Students can prepare by joining their school band. If possible, they may want to take private music lessons, too. As marine musicians must not have stage fright, it would be helpful to become comfortable playing in front of audiences.

★ WHAT IS THE MINIMUM ENLISTMENT TIME FOR MARINE MUSICIANS?

Musicians must sign up to serve in the marine corps for at least four years.

★ HOW SHOULD A CANDIDATE EXPRESS INTEREST IN BEING A MARINE MUSICIAN?

It is best to begin by asking a marine corps recruiter. He or she will connect the candidate with the marines' musical technical assistant or regional placement director. That person not only provides more information but also handles reviewing and auditioning the candidate.

★ WHERE ARE MARINE BAND AUDITIONS HELD?

Auditions for "The President's Own" are held in the John Philip Sousa Band Hall at Marine Barracks Annex in Washington, DC. Auditions for other marine bands are held across the country.

★ WHAT DO MARINE BAND CANDIDATES LEARN AT THE NAVAL SCHOOL OF MUSIC?

Candidates study basic music theory and ear training, marching techniques, and ensemble instruction, along with taking private music lessons. Marine Band members can also return to the school for advanced training.

ESSENTIAL FACTS

US MARINE CORPS HISTORY

- ★ 1775: Marine militias fight from the waterways in the beginning of the American Revolutionary War.
- ★ 1775: The Second Continental Congress officially establishes the US Marine Corps.
- ★ 1800s: Marines fight in a number of small wars.
- ★ 1917: The United States enters World War I and the marines assist in France.
- ★ 1941: Japan attacks Pearl Harbor, Hawaii, and the United States enters World War II, sending many marines to serve in the Pacific.
- ★ 1950: The Korean War breaks out, lasting three years.
- ★ 1954: The Vietnam War begins, with US involvement until 1975.
- ★ 2001: On September 11, terrorists hijack US passenger planes and fly them into New York's World Trade Center, prompting the War on Terror.
- ★ 2000s: Marines combat terrorism in various Middle Eastern countries, including Afghanistan and Iraq, as part of the War on Terror.

US MARINE CORPS ORGANIZATION

The US Marine Corps is part of the US Department of Defense, under the Department of the Navy. Like all members of the US military, marines are organized by rank. Enlisted marines can be divided into junior enlisted ranks, noncommissioned officer ranks, and staff noncommissioned officers. Above these are the commissioned officers, who lead enlisted personnel and make high-level decisions.

CAREER MOVES

How can you prepare for a career in the US Marine Corps?

- ★ Maintain good grades in high school to ensure graduation and to prepare for the exams associated with military training.
- ★ Work to become physically fit.
- ★ Stay healthy, including maintaining healthy eating habits.
- ★ Go online or to a library and research the US Marine Corps or speak with someone who has military experience.
- ★ Go online and research the ASVAB to prepare for taking the military entrance exam.

IMPACT ON SOCIETY

The US Marine Corps has a long history as a premier fighting unit of exceptionally well-trained personnel. The marine corps offers recruits their choice of many career paths with opportunities for growth. There are marines in combat fighting to save lives on the battlefield, intelligence specialists working to gather secret vital information, and Marine Band musicians working to inspire patriotism and support for their fellow marines. The marine corps' motto of being "First to fight" speaks to marines' determination to defend the United States against threats at home and abroad and to protect and assist those in crisis situations.

QUOTE

"I wanted to be a part of something bigger than myself, something that will show me how to succeed and become a better human being."

—Private First Class Brooke L. Jalbert

GLOSSARY

amphibious
Working in both land and water.

aptitude
A natural ability to do something or learn something.

civilian
A person not serving in the armed forces.

deploy
To spread out strategically; to send into battle.

embassy
The official place in a foreign country where an ambassador works to represent his or her country.

enlist
To voluntarily join the military.

fleet
A group of ships that sails together for the same purpose and under one command.

guerrilla warfare
Attacks on civilians and troops by men or women who form their own, unofficial militia.

humanitarian
Concerned with relieving human suffering.

hydraulic systems
A type of technology involving the way liquid moves through pipes to create power or control.

insurgent
A person who fights against a government or other authority.

intelligence
Information that is of military or political value.

marksmanship
The skill of shooting at and hitting a target.

militia
A military force made up of nonprofessional fighters.

polygraph
A device designed for detecting the truthfulness of statements.

struts
Rods or bars that are part of a framework. They help to resist compression, or pushing in, of the frame.

ADDITIONAL RESOURCES

Selected Bibliography

Fabry, Merrill. "How the U.S. Marine Corps Was Founded Twice." *Time*, 10 Nov. 2015. time.com. Accessed 17 Jan. 2020.

"Our Purpose." *Marines*, n.d. marines.com. Accessed 17 Jan. 2020.

"The President's Own." *Marines*, n.d. marineband.marines.mil. Accessed 17 Jan. 2020.

Further Readings

McKinney, Donna B. *US Coast Guard*. Abdo, 2021.

Mooney, Carla. *US Navy*. Abdo, 2021.

Shoup, Kate. *Coding Careers in the Military*. New York: Cavendish Square, 2020.

Online Resources

To learn more about the US Marine Corps, please visit **abdobooklinks.com** or scan this QR code. These links are routinely monitored and updated to provide the most current information available.

More Information

For more information on this subject, contact or visit the following organizations:

Marine Corps Recruit Depot Museum
Day Hall, Building 26
1600 Hochmuth Ave.
San Diego, CA 92140
619-524-6719
mcrdmuseum.org

This museum at the historic San Diego Marine Corps Recruit Depot offers exhibits focused on the history of the US Marine Corps, along with a reference center that includes an archives and research library.

National Museum of the Marine Corps
18900 Jefferson Davis Hwy.
Triangle, VA 22172
877-653-1775
usmcmuseum.com

Visitors can tour this museum online or in person to experience exhibits about the history of the US Marine Corps and the accomplishments of marines.

SOURCE NOTES

CHAPTER 1. MEET THE MARINES

1. "Our Purpose." *Marines*, n.d., marines.com. Accessed 11 Mar. 2020.

CHAPTER 2. THE HISTORY OF THE US MARINE CORPS

1. Merrill L. Bartlett and Jack Sweetman. *The U.S. Marine Corps*. Naval Institute Press, 2001. 23.
2. Claudette Roulo. "Why Are Marines Part of the Navy?" *US Department of Defense*, 21 Feb. 2019, defense.gov. Accessed 11 Mar. 2020.
3. "Marine Corps History: The Medal of Honor." *Military.com*, n.d., military.com. Accessed 11 Mar. 2020.
4. Edwidge Danticat. "The Long Legacy of Occupation in Haiti." *New Yorker*, 28 July 2015, newyorker.com. Accessed 11 Mar. 2020.
5. Stephen S. Evans. *U.S. Marines and Irregular Warfare: 1898–2007*. Marine Corps UP, 2008. 18.
6. Bartlett and Sweetman, *The U.S. Marine Corps*, 133–134.
7. Aaron O'Connell. *Underdogs*. Harvard UP, 2012. 13.
8. O'Connell, *Underdogs*, 1.
9. O'Connell, *Underdogs*, 1.
10. Bethanne Kelly Patrick. "The Montford Point Marines." *Military.com*, n.d., military.com. Accessed 12 Mar. 2020.
11. Brendan Roethel. "Honoring History, Achievements of African American Marines." *US Marine Corps*, 28 Feb. 2017, marines.mil. Accessed 12 Mar. 2020.
12. Robert Trumbull. "40 Years Later, Survivors Gather at Pearl Harbor." *New York Times*, 8 Dec. 1981, nytimes.com. Accessed 11 Mar. 2020.
13. "U.S. Marine Corps Forces Korea: Setting the Force." *Marines*, n.d., marines.com. Accessed 12 Mar. 2020.
14. Bartlett and Sweetman, *The U.S. Marine Corps*, 270–271.
15. Bartlett and Sweetman, *The U.S. Marine Corps*, 274–275.
16. "September 11 Attacks." *History*, 17 Feb. 2020, history.com. Accessed 12 Mar. 2020.
17. J. D. Simkins. "'Combat Obscura' Is a Brutally Honest Look at the Blurred Morality of the War in Afghanistan." *Military Times*, 15 Mar. 2019, militarytimes.com. Accessed 12 Mar. 2020.
18. Phillip Walter Wellman. "'Stop Looking at These Kids as Heroes,' Says Veteran Who Made Documentary Featuring Wartime Footage of Marines." *Stars and Stripes*, 15 Mar. 2019, stripes.com. Accessed 12 Mar. 2020.
19. Stephanie Savell. "This Map Shows Where in the World the U.S. Military Is Combatting Terrorism." *Smithsonian Magazine*, Jan. 2019, smithsonianmag.com. Accessed 12 Mar. 2020.

CHAPTER 3. THE US MARINE CORPS TODAY

1. "Becoming a Marine Overview." *Marines*, n.d., marines.com. Accessed 12 Mar. 2020.

2. Brooke L. Jalbert. "Molly Marine Awardee Essay." *Women Marines Association*, 2 Sept. 2019, womenmarines.wordpress.com. Accessed 12 Mar. 2020.

3. "Recruitment: Marine Corps Training." *Military.com*, n.d., military.com. Accessed 12 Mar. 2020.

4. Lynsey Addario. "Women Becoming Marines." *New York Times*, 24 Mar. 2019, nytimes.com. Accessed 12 Mar. 2020.

5. David Flynn. "Warrant Officer Program Seeks the Best from the Enlisted Ranks." *US Marine Corps*, 16 Dec. 2010, marines.mil. Accessed 12 Mar. 2020.

6. Jon Davis. "What Is It Like to Be a U.S. Marine?" *HuffPost*, 6 Dec. 2017, huffpost.com. Accessed 12 Mar. 2020.

7. Jalbert, "Molly Marine Awardee Essay."

CHAPTER 4. SCOUT SNIPER

1. "Face of Defense: Making Marine Snipers." *US Department of Defense*, 1 July 2019, defense.gov. Accessed 12 Mar. 2020.

2. Lena Sisco. *Marine Scout Snipers*. LP, 2016. 5.

3. "Face of Defense: Making Marine Snipers."

4. Todd South. "A New Sniper MOS? Marines Are Testing a 'Proof of Concept' for Scout Snipers." *Marine Corps Times*, 25 Apr. 2019, marinecorpstimes.com. Accessed 12 Mar. 2020.

5. Shawn Snow. "The Sniper Shortfall." *Marine Corps Times*, 13 Nov. 2018, marinecorpstimes.com. Accessed 12 Mar. 2020.

6. "Face of Defense: Making Marine Snipers."

7. "Face of Defense: One Shot, One Kill." *US Department of Defense*, 2 Oct. 2018, defense.gov. Accessed 12 Mar. 2020.

8. C. J. Chivers. "Perfect Killing Method, but Clear Targets Are Few for Marines in Iraq." *New York Times*, 22 Nov. 2006, nytimes.com. Accessed 12 Mar. 2020.

9. "Face of Defense: Making Marine Snipers."

CHAPTER 5. COUNTERINTELLIGENCE/HUMAN INTELLIGENCE SPECIALIST

1. "Solicitation of Qualified Marines to Lateral Move into the Counterintelligence Human Intelligence PMOS 0211." *US Marine Corps*, 17 Sept. 2018, marines.mil. Accessed 12 Mar. 2020.

2. "Corps Ramps Up Recruiting for Lucrative, Unconventional Intel Jobs." *Military Times*, 8 Oct. 2013, militarytimes.com. Accessed 12 Mar. 2020.

3. "Corps Ramps Up Recruiting for Lucrative, Unconventional Intel Jobs."

4. "How Much Does an E-4 Corporal in the Marine Corps Get Paid?" *Military-Ranks.org*, n.d., military-ranks.org. Accessed 12 Mar. 2020.

SOURCE NOTES CONTINUED

CHAPTER 6. COMBAT PHOTOGRAPHER

1. Tammy Hineline. "Life as a Military Photographer in the U.S. Marines." *Neil van Niekerk: Tangents Photography Blog*, 19 Feb. 2014, neilvn.com/tangents. Accessed 12 Mar. 2020.
2. Hineline, "Life as a Military Photographer."
3. Hineline, "Life as a Military Photographer."
4. Mark Klaas. "Marine from Kent Honored for His Work as a Combat Correspondent, Photographer." *Kent Reporter*, 29 May 2016, kentreporter.com. Accessed 12 Mar. 2020.
5. Stephen M. DeBoard. "Marine Combat Videographer Awarded for Valor." *US Marine Corps*, 18 Feb. 2006, marines.mil. Accessed 12 Mar. 2020.
6. Seth Robson. "Combat Camera Troops Put Their Lives at Risk to Photograph War." *Stars and Stripes*, 23 June 2015, stripes.com. Accessed 12 Mar. 2020.
7. Hineline, "Life as a Military Photographer."

CHAPTER 7. DOG HANDLER

1. "Corporal Christopher Vogt Canine Handler." *Today's Military*, n.d., todaysmilitary.com. Accessed 12 Mar. 2020.
2. American Forces Press Service. "Department of Defense Military Working Dog Program." *Balance Careers*, 29 Sept. 2019, thebalancecareers.com. Accessed 12 Mar. 2020.
3. Shaehmus Sawyer. "Pack Leader: Marine Military Working Dog Handler." *US Marine Corps*, 26 Aug. 2016, marines.mil. Accessed 12 Mar. 2020.
4. Denise K. Sypesteyn. "Canines in Combat: Military Working Dogs." *San Antonio Magazine*, Nov. 2013, sanantoniomag.com. Accessed 12 Mar. 2020.
5. Sawyer, "Pack Leader."
6. "Corporal Christopher Vogt Canine Handler."
7. Edward R. Guevara Jr. "They Have a Nose for Their Business." *US Marine Corps*, 13 June 2003, marines.mil. Accessed 12 Mar. 2020.
8. Peter Tyson. "Dogs' Dazzling Sense of Smell." *PBS NOVA*, 4 Oct. 2012, pbs.org. Accessed 12 Mar. 2020.
9. "Military Working Dogs Finding Their Way Home." *Military Times*, 24 July 2014, militarytimes.com. Accessed 12 Mar. 2020.
10. Aaron Hostutler. "Devildogs, Working Dogs Share Pack Mentality." *US Marine Corps*, 15 Apr. 2010, marines.mil. Accessed 12 Mar. 2020.
11. Bernadette Plouffe. "Behind the Ruff Life of Marine Military Working Dog Handlers and Future K9 Veterans." *USO*, 26 Aug. 2019, uso.org. Accessed 12 Mar. 2020.
12. Plouffe, "Behind the Ruff Life."
13. Plouffe, "Behind the Ruff Life."

CHAPTER 8. AIRCRAFT MECHANIC

1. Tyler Rogoway. "'Absolute Youngest' Marine in the F-35 Test Force Shares His Experiences." *Jalopnik*, 10 July 2015, jalopnik.com. Accessed 12 Mar. 2020.
2. Rogoway, "'Absolute Youngest' Marine."
3. Tyler Ngiraswei. "Marine Corps' Pit Crew: Aircraft Maintenance." *US Marine Corps*, 1 Oct. 2014, marines.mil. Accessed 12 Mar. 2020.
4. Rogoway, "'Absolute Youngest' Marine."
5. "Aircraft Mechanics." *Today's Military*, n.d., todaysmilitary.com. Accessed 12 Mar. 2020.

CHAPTER 9. MARINE BAND MUSICIAN

1. Rachel Ghadiali. "First Female Drum Major to Lead 'The President's Own.'" *US Marine Corps*, 5 June 2017, marines.mil. Accessed 12 Mar. 2020.
2. Chase Baran. "2019 Young People's Concert: The Incredible Big Band." *US Marine Corps*, 1 Apr. 2019, marines.mil. Accessed 12 Mar. 2020.
3. Elliot Lanes. "'A Quick 5' with Master Sergeant David Murry." *MD Theatre Guide*, 19 Apr. 2016, mdtheatreguide.com. Accessed 12 Mar. 2020.
4. "The Commandant's Own." *US Marine Corps*, n.d., marines.mil. Accessed 12 Mar. 2020.
5. Gavin Stewart. "Two from Catawba County Part of Prestigious Marine Drum & Bugle Corps." *Hickory Daily Record*, 22 Dec. 2018, hickoryrecord.com. Accessed 12 Mar. 2020.
6. Stewart, "Two from Catawba County."
7. "Musician Enlistment Option Program." *US Marine Corps*, n.d., marines.mil. Accessed 12 Mar. 2020.
8. Brian Will. "The U.S. Marine Band Has a Rich History of Music." *WSAW TV 7*, 14 Mar. 2019, wsaw.com. Accessed 12 Mar. 2020.
9. Haley Triem. "Marines Are Musicians, Too; Marine Corps Band Plays Voxman." *Daily Iowan*, 16 Apr. 2019, dailyiowan.com. Accessed 12 Mar. 2020.
10. Sophie Erber. "What It Takes to Be in the Marine Corps Band." *TV6 FoxUp*, 4 May 2016, uppermichigansource.com. Accessed 12 Mar. 2020.

INDEX

ABOUT THE AUTHOR

Gail Radley

Gail Radley is the author of nearly 40 books for young people, both fiction and nonfiction, and numerous articles for adults. She also teaches English part-time at Stetson University in DeLand, Florida.